LOVE THE MEDIUMSHIP

BY

JENNI FRAMPTON

COPYRIGHT

ABOUT THE AUTHOR

Jenni is a Clairvoyant Medium based in Hamilton, New Zealand.

An accomplished Spiritual Medium and teacher, she works with Spirit and the Angels to bring hope to where it is needed.

From the age of three and all throughout her life, Jenni was aware of and could talk to people in spirit. Initially apprehensive of the experience and of her ability, she soon came to realise the wonder and ability of her gift.

As well as being a Medium Jenni is also a healer and Registered Celebrant. Jenni also works with spirit through Trance Mediumship. She has done extensive training over the years – honing her ability in mediumship and healing.

Jenni works as a Platform Medium in the many Spiritual churches in New Zealand. She also does private readings and runs workshops and spiritual evenings with her daughter Lyn-Marie Moss who is also an accomplished Medium.

TABLE OF CONTENTS

INTRODUCTION

LOVE THE MEDIUMSHIP, AND I DO.

It's what I was born to do and born to be, a Medium. I love the energy feeling and satisfaction that I get from a good spiritual connection. The sheer joy that I experience when working with Spirit and sharing information with my  clients and my students when I hold classes, deliver readings, or if I am working on platform in Church, or in front of an audience. When I experience the reaction contact with a loved one brings to my client, and see the look of peace and hope when my client leaves after a reading, it makes being a Medium worthwhile. It is a privilege to serve Spirit, and that is what I do.

I have been aware of Spirit from a very early age. It wasn't something I sought or understood; it was just there. I remember my Sunday school teacher saying, "I wish I could do what you can do". I didn't understand what she meant then, because to me it was just talking to God and Spirit, the same as you talk to other living people and animals. It was as natural as breathing; it didn't have a name or a label. It was comfortable, and easy and didn't require any effort. To me it was completely normal.

As a child, I loved going to Church and Sunday School. To me, it was the energy, the feeling of complete faith and the realisation that yes, there was something else out there and if you closed your eyes, it would envelop you, a bit like the feeling of coming home. That feeling would bring you comfort and peace and a feeling of being loved. It was an early form of meditation and prayer and that same feeling has stayed with me for years.

Mediumship is simple if that is what you choose to believe, and I know that it is, so I believe. It does not require flicks of hands, flashing lights, or lowered tones of voice. It is not fear based and should never be approached as such. It is a simple pure link with Spirit to provide proof of life now, and life after life by bringing through information from family and friends that have passed before us to the Spirit world. It comes with love and compassion and is something to treasure, to share and to enjoy. Above all, it is a spiritual connection that brings with it a sense of peace and love.

All it requires from you is trust and faith. Complete trust in Spirit, without whom you cannot do your job as a Medium properly, trust in the knowledge that they will never let you down and the confidence to trust your own ability. Have faith that Spirit always has your back and is there to help you, no matter what the situation is. So strengthen your belief and give permission for Spirit to enhance your day to day living - they will show up when you least expect it. It should, and will, enhance your life and make your days and nights better.

Although Mediumship is classed as a gift, we are all born with the ability to interact with the Spirit world, because that is where we come from, and the ability to develop our mediumship is there, should we choose to do so. This ability comes from the heart and requires empathy and compassion to use it properly. While we all possess this ability, we have the choice of using or denying that gift.

The ability to link with Spirit is often classed as intuition and that is sometimes where the acknowledgement of your gift starts. Depending on your lifestyle or surroundings, peer pressure, and family beliefs the ability can and will dwindle and may potentially be lost but it often resurfaces years down the track.

Mediumship is simply a link from you to someone in Spirit. A link with friends and family that have passed over to Spirit. The link is essentially with your Guides, and your clients Guides, friends, and family. The perfect link is a three-way link, between Spirit and the client with you as the Medium or the middle contact.

Mediums come in all ages, shapes and sizes, and all nationalities, and their abilities are all different as are some of their beliefs. While some Mediums may excel in Trance readings, or Tarot, Spiritual or Psychic readings; it all comes from Spirit, be it from God or the Universe or whatever higher power you believe in, it is still a connection to Spirit.

Some Mediums may work on a Spiritual Church Platform locally or around the world, some at fairs or shows, and some give readings one to one. It all comes down to trust, and the intent and ability of the Medium. The intent of the Medium, and commitment to work with Spirit means that the messages given are exactly the same no matter where the location is.

The Medium's main goal is to contact family and friends in spirit to help people come to terms with grief, after a loved one has died. There is no limit or timeline to a person's grief, they may adjust in a year, or they may never adjust to their loss. Your role as a Medium in this case is to listen and offer words of comfort to your grieving client.

You may have a client who just wants to know where they are heading, are they on the right path, or what lies ahead for them. What you say can provide healing or trauma to someone, so choose your words carefully and listen to what your Guides and your client's Guides are saying. Remember: a good Medium does no harm.

Mediums can be either Spiritual or Psychic, or both. All Spiritual Mediums are psychic as well as spiritual, while a Psychic Medium may follow their intuition more or use tools such as cards, runes or crystals, or some other type of symbol to do a reading.

All Spiritual Mediums are very good spiritual healers. Why, because you are linking to Spirit and asking for spiritual help and assistance to heal your client. You are providing yourself as a healing channel and accepting with faith and trust that this will happen. Remember to always work for the highest good for your client. It is all about the intent and what you believe and want to happen.

A MEDIUM IS SOMEONE WHO CAN CONNECT SPIRITUALLY WITH FRIENDS AND FAMILY WHO HAVE DIED AND PASSED FROM THIS WORLD INTO THE NEXT.

That's it! It is that simple. Nothing scary or negative about it at all. The motto of a good Medium is to do no harm and it is important to remember that always. Do not allow your ego to take over, and let your personal thoughts get in the way. It is not about how wonderful you look or any  fancy words you may use, or how you wish to influence someone, it is about your ability to link with spirit, and your ability to give true messages and proof from your client's loved ones.

Your help is from Spirit, and this is essential as you cannot work without their help. Remember, good mediums are mostly born not made, and require Spirit assistance to help you to become a better medium.

Yes, you can learn the mechanics of being a Medium and the right words to say, but unless it comes from Spirit and from the heart, your heart, it becomes empty words and can do more harm than good. Which is why a Medium requires empathy as well as compassion to help a grieving person and to give an accurate reading and provide much needed healing.

A Medium is a connection or a link to Spirit, a counsellor, listener, healer, advisor, teacher, and many other roles. Sometimes you will be one of the above, sometimes as many as two or three at the same time, which is why it is important to know who to refer people to when they need help that is outside of your abilities. You are not a Doctor and should never give a medical opinion, no matter how tempted you are to do so.

Mediumship is a way of life, not a hobby that you can pick up and put down, and your ability to blend and merge with Spirit will change and expand as you grow in your spiritual awareness. As you become more aware of the existence of Spirit around you, you will find yourself wanting to read more and know more about your own spiritual journey, and that is great, because each journey is different.

Do not compare your progress, learning opportunities, skills and the length of your journey to others. Do not find fault with other Mediums, because their journey, although it seems the same, and has a similar outcome, it will be totally different to yours.

A good Medium has the ability to heal with the words that they say, and also to heal with that special gift of a spiritual healing touch. Again, you are responsible for the words that come out of your mouth, because your words can either heal or damage someone, and your clients will remember your words for years to come. Your words will have an impact on your client, make sure it is positive.

One way to advance your Mediumship, is to find a Spiritual Church in your neighbourhood and see what it has to offer in the way of classes and spiritual support. Spiritual churches are mainly the same, but often subtly different, as they focus on different parts of spirituality.

You will know when you have found the right one, as a feeling of coming home will envelop you when you visit the church or make contact. You will feel as if you are meant to be there and you will find that interacting with likeminded people is always a plus.

PROTECTION IS IMPORTANT

FOR YOU, THE PEOPLE AND THE ANIMALS THAT YOU LOVE.

Of course it is, and for you and your home and family and animals, it is as simple as visualising yourself and those you love in white light or coloured bubbles. You know what a bubble looks like and a bubble can be any size and shape and any colour

and it can change depending on the circumstances.

Put a coloured bubble around your family and friends. You will find that children as they go to school will benefit from this, just get them to choose their favourite colour for the bubble and watch their confidence expand and grow. Listen to your children when they tell you later, how their day went.

But why do you need protection? Do you need protection from Spirit? No, definitely not. Spirit will never harm you, they are there to help you and will always supply strong support and good energy when asked.

Protection is a process of clearing negative energy and can lighten your mood and thoughts, providing a healing energy to all. It can cleanse your aura, your home, your workplace and your surroundings, wherever you are, and it can keep you safe.

I remember years ago when I was taking my grandchildren to the movies and as I was setting out I heard someone in Spirit say "Don't go down Peachgrove Road, go another way." Due to traffic and chatter in the car, I automatically went the fastest way and found myself on Peachgrove Road. Panic, and with no time to change direction I put extra protection around my grandchildren and myself and my car.

A car two cars behind me, was travelling too fast and smashed into the car behind me destroying the whole front of his car and denting the car behind me which was a solid older car. His car bumped into my car leaving a very slight impression of his number plate on my car. No damage to the family and we continued on, a bit shaken but unharmed.

Thank goodness for Spirit protection given willingly to me even though I did not listen and act as I could have. Lesson learned, now I take more notice.

To cleanse your house or workplace of negative energy, simply send white light out to infiltrate and surround your home. This clears out all negative energy which may be there because of arguments, sickness, and other human activities, or the energy may be stale and has settled for too long.

Remember to always send white light out with love and positivity, and to allow it to flow over your boundary to all of your neighbour's boundaries. It is as simple and as quick as a thought.

You can use sage, incense or candles if you want and many people do, but for me white light is stronger, faster and way more effective.

Feeling grumpy and very negative? Try sending love and light to yourself, because it does help. Say this mantra "I love, cleanse and protect myself" and take a deep breath in and out through your nose. If you still don't feel any different then say it again, and again taking a deep breath each time, as many times as you need, and feel your energy and feel-good feelings start to expand and relax you.

Music, especially upbeat music can clear negative energy too. Choose your favourite uplifting music, something that always makes you feel good. Turn the music up loud, feel the rhythm and the beat, and open all the doors and windows to allow fresh air in to uplift and cleanse the energy. It's especially wonderful when you are doing time consuming chores like vacuum cleaning or dusting, to feel the refreshing energy surrounding you and to help you to relax and enjoy the moment.

Read all the books you can find on Spiritualism and Mediumship, and believe only some of the information. The general rule is: if it feels right, then it probably is right. Remember that the book is the author's personal experience and beliefs and his or her way of looking at contact with Spirit may not necessarily be yours, and may not suit your journey.

If there is only one sentence that applies to you, that you believe in or resonate with, then that was all you needed to know in the whole book or series of books. By reading more varied spiritual books, you soon come to realise your own truth.

Never be afraid to learn more and stretch your own information level out, and to question everything that doesn't feel right or sit right with you. Be open to new ideas. What you believe in now, you may not in a few years time, and that's okay because your Mediumship is a growing and changing process. Spirit can help you to understand your gift, and teach you to use your spiritual awareness in the best way possible.

Spirit can only use what you know as a reference. If you have never experienced something or don't know what an object is then Spirit will show you something similar or help you to describe it to your client. Always ask your Guide for help in these situations.

WHAT DOES THIS MEAN AND HOW DO YOU APPLY IT? IS IT NECESSARY? YES, IT IS NECESSARY AND IMPORTANT FOR YOU.

You cannot float in that spiritual space of linking and meditation all the time.

Why not? Yes it feels lovely, like a comfortable cushion, because you are letting life slide past by not making any decisions and that's not good for you. This is your life to live and make your own decisions by being in the moment , being mindful and aware of what is going on around you.

You are a spiritual being having a human existence.

If you are continually linking with Spirit and not doing other things, then you are not having a human existence, are you? That's why grounding is so important for you.

How: There are as many extravagant ideas and options out there of how to ground yourself, almost as many as there are people.

I find the best, the easiest and fastest method is to sit in a chair. It doesn't have to be wooden, fancy, or basic, any chair will do, comfortable is good and I prefer wooden arms on my chair. Intuitively you will know which chair is good for you.

Now, sit comfortably, close your eyes as if you were going to meditate and imagine that your hands, arms and feet are growing down through the floor and into the earth. Sit quietly for a few minutes or so and you will automatically connect to the earth. That feeling of being spaced out or not completely 'with it', will disappear and you will feel better as you ground yourself. This exercise can also be done standing or lying down or wherever you feel comfortable.

You can hug a tree, hold onto the clothesline in the rain, or walk barefoot on the grass. Just do whatever feels good for you and whatever works for you. Keep it simple.

WHY DO YOU NEED ONE? YOU MAY NOT, BUT SOMETIMES IT HELPS TO LEARN THE DIFFERENCE BETWEEN WHAT TO SAY AND HOW TO SAY IT BETTER.

Often you are dealing with vulnerable people, and you don't want the words you say to harm or make someone more upset than necessary.

You will find that Spirit will send you the right teacher at the right time. A good teacher will hone your ability, guide you and help your mediumship expand. They will explain the many different aspects of your spiritual journey to you. Remember it is a journey, not an instant fix, so enjoy the journey and the adventures on which you are being taken. Take it day by day and a moment at a time and above all relax and enjoy every step.

I had the best teacher ever, when starting out as a practising medium. Her name was Jen and there wasn't anything that she couldn't help with, explain, or show a better way of linking with Spirit. Her classes were great as were her trance sessions. She taught us to look outside the obvious and to always trust Spirit.

I also went to the Arthur Findlay College in Stanstead, England to expand my knowledge, which I did, and loved the experience. This is something I would recommend if you can afford the time and the cost. It was very enjoyable and I met some lovely likeminded people from all over the world and I learnt a lot of new ways of doing mediumship.

You may not agree with what your teacher tells you or the way that he or she encourages you to work. Just use it as an experience. Never disrupt or continually bring in what a previous teacher told you unless it is an appropriate time or message. Remember you are there to learn and if it is not right for you, then move on. There is always a reason.

Practice with your friends, and give them a reading. Make sure you are linking properly with Spirit and not just using your knowledge about your friend to give them a message.

Be sure that the information given is true and not just what you wish it to be, or what your friend wants it to be. Always strive to make each reading better and more accurate than the last one. Ask your Guide to help you to be 100% accurate, or as close to this as you can be.

Always strive to be the best medium that you can be.

Being the best medium you can be means that you will always grow in your awareness of Spirit, and that you will expand what you know about mediumship and your connection to Spirit. Don't ever be complacent, always question everything, because this attitude will help you to become better at what you do.

You want to be the best Medium you can be. Not the best in the world, that's ego and you don't want or need that. Being a good Medium is to serve Spirit to the best of your ability and to always help other people and to love and respect the animals and other inhabitants of this earth.

Parts of your journey to be a Medium will race by and then you may feel as if you are marking time and not getting anywhere fast enough, and nothing is happening. Are you racing through your experiences with Spirit without fully understanding what is happening around you and to you? Look around you, perhaps you are subconsciously waiting for your knowledge to expand and deepen. Do you sometimes feel as if you have taken one or two steps backwards?

In that situation, try meditating and asking your Guides and Spirit for help and go back to basics and start again. What are you not doing, and what is missing? It may just be that the timing is not ready for you yet.

Are all the readings that you are doing appearing to be the same, do people seem to have the same problems and do you find yourself repeating your words with each reading?

This is common and it may be a lesson from Spirit teaching you to understand better what you are experiencing and saying. Should you be using a better choice of words? Should you be asking more questions from Spirit? Are you just skimming the surface ie: where and what is the proof from the person in Spirit for your client and you?

It all takes time. Sometimes you need to repeat a lesson in order for you to gain a better knowledge and an understanding of what you are experiencing. Don't forget that Spirit sends the right client to you, at the right time, because you are the medium that they need at that time.

Learn your basic Mediumship linking skills well and go back to your basic knowledge if you are having trouble. Are you linking in properly with Spirit, or are you guessing, hoping you have it right, and falling short of your ability. It's all about timing and experience.

WHY DO WE HAVE OR WHY DO WE NEED A SPIRITUAL GUIDE? BECAUSE OUR LIVES WOULD NOT BE THE SAME WITHOUT ONE. WE NEED THEIR HELP TO EXIST IN A BETTER WAY AND TO EXPERIENCE MORE OPPORTUNITIES IN THIS WORLD OF OURS.

We all have a Master spiritual guide, they may present themselves as just energy, female or male. Master spiritual guides have linked with us before we were born. They were assigned to us and were there helping us to decide where we were going to  be born and the experiences in life that we wanted or needed to have. Sort of like a basic road map with important dates, times and choices marked out, leaving you to colour your life and your map as you wish, and however you choose.

Your Master Guide is always with you until you pass back to the spirit realm, helping to keep you on your path, assisting you daily and advising you of upcoming opportunities.

Although they are there to help with any decision you make in life, they are not there to make the decisions for you. It is up to you how well you handle your life's journey and what you put into it and get out of it, because this is your life, no-one else's. Remember that you have free will and you are responsible for your own actions and words.

During your life span on Earth other Guides will come in and out of your life's journey, sometimes for a short period of time and sometimes they will stay for many years. Their role is a specialist role to help you with new projects and different ways of life. The same as you would go to a swimming instructor or learn Pilates or hypnotherapy or a different way of healing. You will notice when a new Guide is coming as there is a feeling of change or unrest around you. Just accept that this feeling will pass and your energy will soon settle down.

Ask your Guide for help in all life's problems and choices, large or small. Job interviews, parking, health problems, financial or relationship problems, nothing is too small or too large. The Guides are there to help you to find the best path, in order for you to have the best outcome.

Learn to trust your Guide because they have your best interests at heart. Look out for signs that they are around you. It may be as simple as a feeling or noticing an article in a magazine, newspaper or a tv programme.

Your Guides cannot live your life for you because you choose your own path, but they are there to help and advise you on anything and everything. Your Guides will never harm you or advise you to harm yourself or others. They will encourage you on your path and teach you how to protect yourself from any negative energy that has been created around you.

Remember to always be grateful and thank your Guide for their help with your day and especially for any help during a reading. Saying thank you to your Guide and Spirit closes a reading by disconnecting the link and allows you to move on to the next person. It also shows Spirit that you recognise them by showing your gratitude for their help.

WHAT IS A MEDIUM? A MEDIUM IS A PERSON WHO LINKS WITH THE SPIRIT REALM, FRIENDS, AND FAMILY IN SPIRIT TO PROVIDE PROOF OF LIFE AFTER LIFE. TO ALSO SHOW PROOF THAT SPIRITS ARE AROUND US IN OUR DAILY LIVES.

How does a Medium work? A medium talks to spirits, guides and loved ones who have passed, providing a link for the client through clairvoyance,  clairaudience, or clairsentience to receive information. Hence the title Medium.

Connection, or linking to Spirit may be shown in many other ways, including music, symbols, trance, spiritual art, and healing. The medium gradually moves to the clair that they feel comfortable with.

There are essentially three types of mediums:

Clairvoyant: Is a Medium that can see people, animals, and Angels in spirit. They can describe to you the person that they see, what they are wearing, the colour of their hair etc. A Clairvoyant sometimes sees Spirit in colour, but often in black and white or Sepia.

They will see the physical body of people in spirit, either in their "mind's eye", or standing beside them. They may also see Spirit as a hologram, a shadow or as a shimmering energy beside or in front of them.

Clairaudient: This type of Medium can hear what Spirit is saying in different ways. Messages are sometimes heard directly in your ear, as a physical voice, a song, a tune or music in your head. Spirit often conveys messages this way. Sometimes a thought can be a clairaudient message from Spirit. This is sometimes the last sense to develop that the medium is aware of.

Clairsentient: a clairsentient is a Medium who can sense or feel the energy of spirit around them, often felt as a warmth or a feeling that someone is there. This is often the first gift to surface and grows rapidly as the Medium advances in ability and confidence.

The Medium is aware of and can feel changes in energy and temperature when someone in spirit is close or around them. They have a feeling, which is often described as knowing and can be related to or mistaken for intuition.

Do you need all three abilities to link with Spirit?

The answer is no; you only need one. Most people start with sensing the presence of spirit, feeling the change of energy and the awareness of someone around them. Some Mediums think that they only have one good ability, but that's not correct. Eventually all three gifts roll into one as the Medium advances in knowledge and grows in their linking ability, and it then becomes a knowing or a deep confident understanding.

Take ownership of your Mediumship and remember that you are responsible for the words that come out of your mouth. Realise that words are very powerful, they can either lift and give peace and motivation, or they can hurt and destroy or damage your client's beliefs or feelings. Your words can influence people into doing good things, taking chances, or not, especially if your ego gets in the way, and you allow your personal feelings to interfere with your reading.

You may be a combination of all three types of Medium, or you may work predominantly with one. You may initially be stronger in one ability than the others but over time you may find that all three senses will blend into one. Good Mediumship comes from the heart and a strong link to Spirit.

Clair- delusion: Not a Medium type and you certainly don't want to be one of these. This person uses a great deal of imagination and is usually very gifted with words using their ability as an entrepreneur to advance. Often very charismatic and believable, with a super ego, this person can do a lot of harm, while professing to offer great advice. In all my years of teaching I have only ever come across a couple of individuals in my classes who fit this role. In fact, this word is now banned in my classes.

There are however a few so-called Mediums out in the community who unfortunately fit this description and they can do more harm than good as their ability is based on their own ego and their intent is to help themselves rather than help other people.

FIND A GOOD TEACHER AND JOIN A GROUP OF LIKE-MINDED PEOPLE. IT CAN BE EITHER A TEACHING CLASS OR A CIRCLE. IN MY EXPERIENCE A TEACHING CLASS IS BETTER, BUT YOU MAY ENJOY THE RELAXED COMPANY IN A CIRCLE.

Join a spiritual Church and find help from there. Your Guide will help with this. You will know when you have found the right place for you to grow your ability, because you will experience a feeling like coming home.

Every teacher is different and will approach linking with spirit initially on how they were taught and on their own life experiences. Sometimes you will be inspired to change your teacher or move on. Follow that instinct because it is your Guide's way of showing you another way of learning, and another level to build your mediumship to.

Learn to trust your ability and to trust your Guide, because he or she will help you to expand your knowledge. Ask for your Guide's help to expand your awareness. Love what you are doing and remember that no-one is perfect. It all takes time.

Practice, practice, practice.

Practice with your friends and family. Practice linking to spirit and trust and believe in what you are hearing.

Try this Exercise

Link into Spirit and do a reading for yourself and write it down. Write down who is talking to you from Spirit: is it your Guide or a loved one. Ask for proof and as much information and guidance that you can get. Don't forget to date it. Put it aside and come back to it in a few months to test your accuracy, and to see if Spirit's information and guidance has come true.

Do a yearly prediction chart for yourself.

Manifest and visualise all the things and all the opportunities you would like to happen for you in the coming year.

Using an A4 or A2 sheet of paper, fill the page up with words and pictures from magazines that advertise what it is that you would like to happen or come into your life. Hang it somewhere so you can see it every day, the back of your wardrobe door is a good place, making it easier for you to affirm what it is you want out of life.

Learn how to switch your linking with Spirit on and off: you are either working with Spirit or not working. If you are not sure how to switch off, then imagine a very old light switch from years back, one that you move up and down. See this in your mind's eye and see the switch being turned up or down by you.

Why should you switch off? Because you are a spiritual being having a human existence, and you are here on this earth to enjoy and learn from your human experiences.

Discipline yourself as this will make your Mediumship ability better. It will also help you to focus better, remember one thing at a time and one day at a time. Don't be that nosy Medium who has to know what is happening to other people, every minute of the day.

Realise that you are not a Fortune Teller. You are a spiritual being having a human experience, and you are a Medium. So, while occasionally Spirit may give you advice relating to the future, it can be changed by the client.

It is your clients choice, and they may choose not to listen to your words, or your client may take notice of your words and change their life journey. Either way is ok, because that moment had been programmed already into their life plan.

Listen to what your Guide is telling you and give the information to your client no matter how random or unbelievable it may seem.

I remember once where the father in Spirit was trying to tell his daughter that he was often around her, on car journeys and interaction with others and she had trouble comprehending and was very sceptical. He said to me "tell her about the Wonky Donkey" so I did, half expecting my client to think I'd lost the plot and I'm sure that's exactly what she thought.

It didn't make any sense to her until halfway through the reading, when she suddenly said "I was reading that book to my granddaughter in the car the other day. How wonderful that my Father was there and listening too." Providing the proof that he was there at the reading. So remember to always give to your client what you hear from Spirit unless it could be harmful.

Remember the golden words

A good Medium does no harm. Your job as a Medium is to inspire and give your client hope for the future and provide proof from the past. To provide proof that friends, and family have not left forever, they are still around for us to talk to. You are not there for an ego trip. It is a way of life and once you have experienced it you will never look back. Always look for Spirit help and work in the light.

As a Medium you are a listener, advisor, counsellor, teacher, and healer as well as a channeler to loved ones in Spirit. Having a list of people and professional contacts to give to your client would be beneficial. Some clients may need help that is outside of your scope, be it medical, legal or another type of spiritual awareness.

You are not a Doctor, so avoid giving medical advice, instead suggesting a checkup with the appropriate Doctor or eye specialist, or dentist etc may help.

Try not to frighten your client by saying the wrong thing and watch your wording because if there is one negative bit of information given, your client will hear it and dwell on it sometimes for years afterwards.

I remember being asked about thirty years ago by a medium if I was married to my second husband yet. I was happily married to my first, which caused a bit of anxiety at the time. She also told me I was going to win a major lotto amount of money, and win a house. I'm still waiting for all three to occur.

So, how do you link to Spirit

If you are wondering how to link then you are probably more than halfway there and already linking. You may have sensed someone beside you, or caught a glimpse of someone out of the corner of your eye. Because it all comes down to feelings, what you sense and are aware of. Can you feel someone around you, can you sense or can you see someone there?

What can you hear? Is there music in your head? Can you hear certain songs whenever you are near someone? Can you smell perfume, flowers, musty old clothes, cigarette or cigar smoke, or perhaps petrol?

I remember one of my ex students telling me that her husband sat up in bed one night and said "Did you hear that? I think there's someone there, not a real person, but a spirit or a ghost".

She turned to him and said "Remember when we were in class, and what Jenni said to ask someone in Spirit ".

Just ask:

"Who are you and what is your name? Why are you here and what do you want?"

There may be times when you sense or feel someone around you or in the corner, and maybe you feel uneasy, then ask the questions.

"Who are you and what is your name?

Why are you here and what do you want?"

Don't be afraid because Spirit will not harm you, just ask the questions and wait for the answers. Don't sit there shivering, be bold and ask questions. Your Guide will help you to not let the opportunity to connect to Spirit pass you by.

MEDITATION

MEDITATION IS SIMPLY THE ACT OF SITTING QUIETLY TO COMMUNE WITH SPIRIT AND WITH YOURSELF. MEDITATE DAILY OR TWICE DAILY FOR AT LEAST 10 MINUTES PER TIME, 20 MINUTES OR LONGER IF YOU CAN MANAGE IT.

This activity helps you to clear your head and to zone out, because the zoning out will help you link better with your Guide. Meditation will help not only your mediumship by giving it more depth and a better understanding, but will also help you in your day  to day living. It will give you time to zone out and make plans subconsciously for your day ahead.

Prepare yourself by making sure that you are not going to be interrupted or startled suddenly by an animal, the phone, or a person knocking on the door or coming into the room.

How... Begin by placing your feet flat on the floor, making yourself comfortable and putting yourself into a quiet meditative state by relaxing and breathing deeply.

Time the meditation, and say to your Guide "I only want to meditate 10 minutes today". While some people find that lying down is a comfortable way to meditate, I don't. For me, I find lying down to meditate a lot harder unless I need it to help me sleep.

Link in to all the sounds that are around you, such as traffic, birds and other familiar noises. You can use music, but this doesn't always help as you may find that you will listen to the music and not always to Spirit.

It may at the start, because it helps you to clear your mind and teaches you to focus. So, take it slowly, if it doesn't work for you the first time then try again and again until you are happy with your control over your breathing and state of mind.

I find that pan flutes can take me to that place of relaxation, but everyone is different, so if it helps, find relaxing music that you love and have it playing softly in the background.

You can join a group to help with your meditation or practice on your own. The choice is yours. Meditate at the same time every day if you can, because this sets a pattern with Spirit and makes it easier for you, but there are no fixed rules.

The more you meditate, the faster it is to zone out and link to Spirit. Practice breathing slower and deeper until you have really good results.

Remember to breathe deeply and to have a drink of water before and after the meditation to help your body refresh. This is good for your physical health as well.

Try this meditation exercise

Read it out loud or get someone else to read it and record it. When you are ready, push play on your phone or whatever you have recorded this meditation on, relax and enjoy.

It's one of my meditations.

Out of a dream.

Please sit comfortably with your feet flat on the floor and prepare to come on a journey with me. Wriggle a bit to make sure you are comfortable and close your eyes. Take a deep breath in and slowly release it. Breathe in and out again and relax knowing that you are in a safe place.

Imagine you are in a beautiful room in an ancient castle on top of a hill, in a far, far- away land. Everywhere you look and everything you see is magnificent, beautiful, and slightly unreal, yet comforting in a strange way. There are ancient red tapestries with gold and blue trimmings around the edges, that are hanging off the stone walls. The furniture is like something you have seen in an old movie, but it has a warm comfortable feeling to it as if you have been here before. It is very welcoming and very peaceful.

Walk over to the window area and find yourself a comfortable seat there, where you can look out and see the hills and along the shores of the island. The scenery is very beautiful and has a calming effect on you. The sky is a grey blue colour, and the sun is slowly rising. It is promising to be a day full of answers and solutions for you. Breath in the fresh salty air and think about what you want most in life while you wait for your Guide.

Your Guide has arrived bringing your friends and family with him. You feel the love and the warmth that comes from those in spirit around you. Sit a while and listen while they talk. Listen also to the words of your Guide as he or she reminds you what you are here for and gives you a plan and encouragement for the future. Do not be disheartened if you do not understand immediately, for it will all be clear in time as it is meant to be.

I will leave you here for a while to talk.

Wait for a few minutes, pause then continue...

All too soon it is time to leave. You have the sensation of everything and everyone fading around you, but do not worry you can return at any time you wish, just ask spirit.

When you are ready, wriggle your fingers and toes, take a deep breath, and come back to your seat in the room.

Welcome back and I hope you enjoyed your meditation.

THIS IS A MUCH DEEPER TYPE OF LINKING TO SPIRIT, SIMILAR TO A MEDITATION AND IT REQUIRES A BIT OF PLANNING AND A LOT OF FOCUS AND DISCIPLINE.

As with meditation: find a quiet place where you will not be interrupted. Plan the time with Spirit and allow yourself 20 minutes, making sure phones are off and no-one is likely to startle you, i.e. animals, children, or visitors.

A comfortable seat with good back support that you will not fall off as you relax further into the meditation. You do not want music or any distraction while you are sitting in the power. It is a communication with Spirit where you will enhance your mediumship and learn to trust and work with your Guides. It is a time of questions and answers.

Remember to breathe deeply at the start and to continue to breathe deeply through the sitting. Have water available when you finish and make sure you are warm enough during your sitting. If you feel cold when you come out of your deep relaxation, then a hot sweet drink will always help, as will chocolate.

Try this Exercise

Have paper beside you to write down anything that you remember afterwards, or you can record on your phone. This is your time to work with your Guides once or twice a week to hone your mediumship and healing abilities, because Mediumship and Healing often go hand in hand.

TRANCE IS A NATURAL PROGRESSION FROM SITTING IN THE POWER WHICH MAY APPEAL TO YOU.

As with all other forms of Mediumship, you may just absorb yourself into it and love it.

You may find that it is not for you and that's okay, there are many other forms of Mediumship to choose from that will suit your ability.

You will need to form or join a group of likeminded people to have success with trance, as you rely on other people's energy to help your trance energy advance properly. A group of five or six people who can meet regularly, every week or two-week intervals, is a good number. As well as this, you will need someone in the group to watch and record any changes so that your ability can be monitored.

Make sure you and your group are warm enough, because trance can cause the body temperature to drop especially if there is a "physical" Medium sitting.

Alternatively, you may find that your room becomes very hot if your sitter is a healer.

Have plenty of water in the room for your group to drink, and for you also when you have finished your trance sitting. Keep it simple, your Guide is aware fully of what is planned and is there for protection.

Your Guide and the "sitter's" Guide will be there to act as gatekeepers to protect the "sitters" energy, so that they don't overdo the sitting. Start off with 15-20 minutes per sitting, and gently encourage the medium to breathe deeply and slowly go into a deeper meditation. Bring the medium (sitter) back gently to awareness of being in the room should they show any signs of distress. It may be that they have become too cold or are not blending well with the energy at that time. Your Guide will tell you as well, and will give you a heads-up and the reason why. Bring the medium's energy back slowly into the room, and get them to sit quietly. Give them water to drink, either hot or cold depending how they are feeling.

As a Medium becomes more comfortable with trance, they will sit for an hour or two, which is why it is important to watch breathing, temperature and any other signs.

An experienced Trance Medium, with healing abilities, will often send healing to all in the room while they are in a trance state. The room will become very warm and you will all receive healing. It may be hard to stay awake while this is happening. The medium may talk at this stage and offer advice.

Alternatively, a Medium who is a strong physical medium will connect at a much deeper depth and has the ability to chill the room in order to link with spirit. This takes years of practice, not so much to achieve it but to stay safe. It is always advisable to have water on hand and a blanket and something sweet, chocolate is always good.

Look after your sitters and helpers who are having their energy used by the main sitting Medium. Make sure that they can sit quietly without talking, for an hour or so, and make them comfortable and warm while they sit. Everyone should have water to drink and blankets ready if the temperature suddenly drops.

Allow no interruptions and switch all phones off and monitor the medium sitting and the support group of mediums.

Try to sit regularly and at the same time of day, fortnightly or weekly is good because you are making an appointment with Spirit to assist you in your trance episodes. This will make your trance work stronger and help you to go to a deeper level linking to Spirit.

EXERCISES TO ASSIST YOUR PSYCHIC READINGS

THESE EXERCISES FALL INTO THE PSYCHIC ABILITY AND AWARENESS BRACKET.

They expand your spiritual awareness by moving your boundaries and allowing Spirit to see how you work, and what you know.

Remember that Spirit can only use what you know. If it is something that you have not seen before, then ask spirit to help you to describe it.

They will work with symbols to help you understand what it is that you see, feel, or hear. Some Mediums have trouble with the Psychic side, and that's okay. They prefer to link directly to Spirit rather than to use tools and Spirit will allow for that and find you another path to help you learn more.

If the energy from your client's person in Spirit is very strong, then ask for the energy to be changed to be easier to connect with. It is ok to ask your Guide to bring someone else through whose energy is more compatible with your energy.

Try this exercise

See if you are understanding a little of how Mediumship works:

Close your eyes and imagine a bright green apple.

See it in your mind's eye. Turn it around and look at it. How would you describe it? Is it whole or blemished?

Touch it. Is it soft to touch? Is it very hard? Does it still have the stalk in it? Is the colour all it should be?

Smell it, what does it smell like? What does it remind you of, good times, family, hard times or love and laughter?

Take a big bite. What does it taste like? Is it sweet, sour, tasteless or a bit mushy, how would you describe it?

Well done! You have experienced a part of Mediumship and your first step forward to being the Medium you would like to be.

You have used your knowledge of what an apple should be like and taken it further by building on your memory and using all your senses and linking with Spirit for answers. Remember, Spirit uses your memory of objects or people, to help with a reading.

Try this exercise

Your symbol is two linked gold rings.

As before, close your eyes, go into a small meditation and link with these rings and Spirit to do a reading. Ask your Guide for help during this lesson.

Concentrate on the rings and ask these questions.

Why are there two rings and why are they linked?

Is one bigger than the other, or are they bent out of shape? Are they worn out, or shiny and new, or does one look new and one not?

How many people have owned the rings and how many people wore them?

Are they passed down from family or friends, or did you buy them?

Who do they remind you of?

The questions are yours. Ask your Guide for help.

Write all the information down or record it as you are given it. Do not go into a practice reading with an idea of who this is for, just trust Spirit to give you the answers. Write down all the information you are given from Spirit.

When you have finished writing, you will know who the message is for and you will be surprised by the amount of information that has been given to you. Sometimes that reading is for yourself, and it may be your Guide's way of helping you to practise.

If the information is for someone else, be sure to ask their permission before passing it on. Not everyone wants information from the past or the future, because not everyone believes in Spirit or wants to hear about it. It may be against their beliefs or religion. Respect other people's points of view and opinions.

SYMBOLS ARE OFTEN GIVEN BY SPIRIT TO ASSIST YOU WITH YOUR READING AND TO PROVIDE DEPTH AND UNDERSTANDING FOR YOUR CLIENT.

As with the flower, use the colours and meaning of your symbol to assist you. Some clients like to see an object such as a Tarot card or Rune stone as it gives them something to focus on.

Spirit can only use your knowledge or understanding of an object or thing to provide proof for your client. This is often shown as a picture in your head. If you don't understand what is being shown, ask your Guide for more proof, and then describe the object to your client.

See what you can do with these examples.

Looking at each of these pictures individually, what is the first thing you think of?

Using all the previous examples that you worked through, try this: How do these objects relate to you and what can you tell me about them?

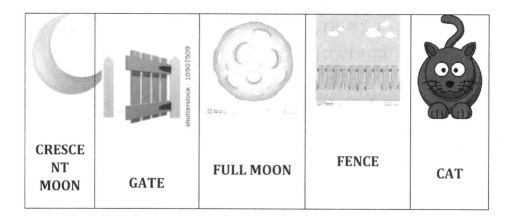

CRESCENT MOON	**GATE**	**FULL MOON**	**FENCE**	**CAT**

SCRYING IS USING A TOOL TO HELP YOU TO FOCUS, YOU MAY SEE PICTURES OR FACES AND MANY TOOLS FALL INTO THIS CATEGORY.

It is the ability to use and look into any object, crystal, candle, ribbon, mirror, clouds or cards to assist your Psychic ability and help make your readings stronger and more accurate.

It can become a crutch if you let it, but you will get to the stage where it is no longer needed. It should only be used as an aid and is often used as confidence for the reader and provides something for your client to see.

There is a huge variety to choose from, crystal balls, cards and pendulums also fall into this category.

Types of Scrying:

There are many different types of scrying, as many as your imagination sends you and as many as your Guide gives to you to try. Try them all and choose the ones that appeal to you. They are all different and help you to focus better on your Mediumship.

Did you ever wonder about people centuries ago who used the living room fire to scry and predict from, just by staring into the flames and seeing things and events happening in there. No TV and an abundance of time certainly helped them to predict the future, and to set the path for future mediums to follow.

PICK A FLOWER, ANY TYPE OF FLOWER
TO DO YOUR READING, WHATEVER
APPEALS TO YOU.

Look at your overall flower, the colour of it, and the strengths and weaknesses of the flower. Does it have a long stem, or a short one, is the stem woody or crooked, perhaps thicker at one end. How can you describe it and relate this to your client?

Does it shine by day and hide in the night?

Does it have a perfume that makes you feel happy, alert, or positive or no perfume at all?

Does it have many petals or only a few, are they evenly numbered, or does the flower have prickles that stab you.

Is it beautiful, cultivated, rare, grown in the wild or on the seashore? Use all aspects of the flower to do your reading.

Relate what you see and everything that you feel to your client. Always ask your Guide for help and listen for the answers as they may observe something that you have missed.

CANDLE READING

CHOOSE A CANDLE, ANY SHAPE AND
SIZE WILL DO, FROM TEALIGHT
CANDLES TO THE VERY LARGE CHURCH
CANDLES.

Looking into the flame of a candle, focusing on what is inside the flame, and by concentrating hard you can experience some amazing results. It puts you into a meditative state allowing you to blend with spirit to provide depth to your reading.

Use the light of the candle flame and the strength and colour of this flame to help you with your reading. Has the flame split in two? Does it have more than one colour? Are the flames even or is one stronger than the other?

What do you think that this means? What can you see when you look into the depths of the flames?

What are you thinking of and are you hearing or seeing anything other than just flames?

Use your intuition and relate it to your client and tell them what you see.

CRYSTAL BALL

ANY TYPE OF CRYSTAL, AND ANY
COLOUR, SIZE AND SHAPE WILL DO FOR
YOUR CRYSTAL BALL.

It can be a large clear round object, or a smaller crystal ball with colourful objects such as flowers inside it, or even a snow globe can be used effectively.

This exercise, as with all scrying, is to focus on the centre of the ball, almost as if you were looking through it for any information that it will give you.

So what can you see, more symbols perhaps? Objects, people or colour, or nothing at all? What are you feeling? What are you thinking?

Don't be disheartened, it all takes time and practice and lots of focus. Even if you can't see anything immediately, just give it time and keep looking. Again, practice practice, practice.

Besides, different types of crystal balls are not only a useful tool but can be beautiful ornaments to look at on your shelf.

Allow your Guide to help you, and as always ask Spirit for assistance. Use the information you glean to assist you with your reading for your client.

THERE ARE MANY DIFFERENT TYPES OF CRYSTALS, AND ALL HAVE DIFFERENT ABILITIES TO BOTH HEAL AND TO BE USED AS A PSYCHIC TOOL.

Choose a crystal that waves at you, or shines brightly attracting your attention, and wanting you to pick it up.

What is attracting you to this crystal, is it the colour or shape, and do you know what its properties are?

Is the crystal warm or cold to hold? Do you want to keep holding it, or do you immediately want to put it down, and why? How does it make you feel?

If you are using crystals for a reading for your client, then get your client to pick the crystal. Always give your client the choice. So why did they choose that particular one? Was it the colour or the shape? How do they feel when they are holding the crystal?

Should your client wear this particular crystal for confidence or healing? Or should it be around them more in their everyday lives.

Crystal readings are fun and a bit different to crystal ball readings, so enjoy the variety and explore the difference between the many crystals that you have. You can never have too many crystals, they all have their place in your life's work.

READING WITH A MIRROR

THIS IS AN EXERCISE THAT IS FUN WITH MORE THAN ONE PERSON.

The object of it is to deepen your awareness of what is around you and strengthen your linking to Spirit.

Sit down in a quiet place and make yourself comfortable. Use a hand mirror and scry into it, concentrating on looking past your reflection and seeing what may be there behind you. A medium size mirror that you can hold comfortably is the best tool to use.

In order for this exercise to work properly, a meditative state is required for the best results.

Who can you see? Is anyone there? Can you see your Guide, someone from your family, or an old friend that has passed to Spirit, or maybe an old pet animal?

Can you see objects from family life, or a memory? Use it all for practice in your linking to Spirit, because that is one of the ways that Spirit helps you.

See if you can do a reading for someone else with this exercise.

USING COLOUR TO ASSIST YOU WITH YOUR READINGS CAN BE VERY HELPFUL IN A VARIETY OF WAYS.

It allows you to work more confidently, because you are concentrating on the colours and not on the person you are reading for.

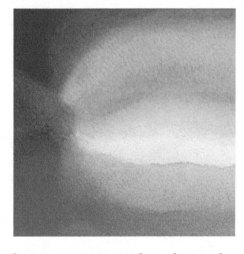

Use of colour cards, ribbons or photos comes into this category. The objects can be any colour, shape or size, multicoloured or single, shiny and glittery. You can do a reading from any of these objects.

TAKE A VARIETY OF RIBBONS, LONG, SHORT, THIN, WIDE, BRIGHT, OR SUBTLE, THEY ALL HAVE A MESSAGE.

What does the colour remind you of?

Do you want to go places with this colour or does it trigger a memory that may help your client?

Is the ribbon straight and smooth, multi coloured, or does it have a thick or fine edge? Is it flecked or uneven in colour, or maybe dull, tatty, or is it shiny? Is it a really long ribbon, or is it short and stubby?

Should your client be wearing more of a particular colour? How can it help them in their daily life? Do they need a colour for healing?

Why did you choose this particular ribbon, and how does it relate to your client?

What is all of this telling you and what is the message from Spirit that you are receiving?

POSTCARD OR COLOUR CARD READINGS

OLD POSTCARDS OR USED BIRTHDAY CARDS ARE USEFUL TOOLS.

Use the colours in the card as a link and delve deeply into it to see what information it presents, whether it is to do with advice from spirit or a Guide, or healing. It may give you an insight into what is happening around your client.

Focus on the objects: is there someone behind that tree, an orb in the corner, or maybe an animal. Is Spirit waving at you from this picture?

Look at the words, if any, on the cards. What do they remind you of? How do they make you feel?

Use all the information you get to give you more assistance for your reading.

Remember to listen while you look into the postcard as there may be additional information given to you from someone in Spirit, either as spoken words or sometimes you may hear music playing.

YOU MAY BE GIVEN A PHOTO OF SOMEONE WHO HAS PASSED TO SPIRIT.

Look carefully at the photo and tune into the photo to find out all you can about this person.

Who are they, and where did they live on Earth? What is their relationship to you or your client? Did they have family or animals?

What type of person were they and what was their personality? Were they loving, grumpy, friendly to others, talkative, selfish, mean. Were they helpful and supportive and did they love and care about your client?

What was their role here on Earth and at what age did they pass. How did they pass, old age, natural causes, perhaps an accident. Did they die suddenly or was it a long drawn out illness?

Allow yourself to relax and link with the energy of the photo in front of you to gather accurate information for your client.

PAST, PRESENT AND FUTURE DRAWINGS

THESE TWO EXERCISES CAN BE USED
FOR YOUR SPIRITUAL EXPANSION, AND
TO SHOW YOU HOW TO GIVE MORE
DEPTH TO A READING.

The way you approach it is only limited by your imagination. You may do this for a client or for yourself. By allowing your imagination freedom, you will surprise yourself with your ability to tune into Spirit.

Try this exercise

Draw a picture to cover your page, using A4 paper. You will find that the portrait view is best, but landscape works as well. When you have finished your drawing, fold your paper lengthwise into three partitions.
Your past is the left portion,
your present is in the middle and
your future is on the right.
Focus on the colour and content of each section and use this to do your own personal reading. What

information can you glean from each portion of your drawing and how can you turn this into a reading?

Try this exercise

Draw a large circle covering your A4 page. Again, using a portrait view, fill your circle up with words and sayings, photos or mini drawings.
Use the example and method quoted previously, divide and fold your paper into three lengthwise. You now have your past, present and future reading waiting for you.

Using either one of the previous examples, provide some depth to your reading by putting a small glass over the part of your picture that stands out to you, and expand and draw that mini part on another paper, and do another reading from that. You can do this as many times as you like, by using your glass and going into each mini picture, taking a segment and making a larger picture. Then do a reading from your next drawing.

These exercises will help you to focus and will allow Spirit to assist you in a different way by giving you more depth, clarification and expansion in your readings. Compare each of the readings that you have done from the same drawing and parts of. Have you gained a better and deeper understanding of the process?

THIS EXERCISE FALLS UNDER THE CATEGORY OF SCRYING, AND CAN BE GREAT FUN.

It involves linking with Spirit to see where your client's spirit family has lived previously and where they worked.

This exercise is very good in helping you to understand more by practising with another person. It delves into your client's memory of their childhood and interaction with their family.

Again, go into a meditative state and walk through the gate of your client's Spirit family home and describe it to your client.

Focus on what you are seeing, sensing and hearing.

Is the property large or small and is it fenced? What type of fence, brick, wooden, metal?

What is the pathway or driveway like, is there one? Is it narrow or wide, stepping stones, dirt or just a grass area?

Go in through the front door, what colour is it? What type of door, is it wooden, glass, single or double? Does it open in or out, or does it slide?

Is there a passageway, how many bedrooms and what does the lounge and kitchen look like? Are there any other rooms, is there a porch?

Describe all of this to your client, and don't forget the outside of the property. Are there any sheds? Can you see the clothesline, what type is it? What can you see over the back fence

In your meditation, wander around and take note of what you can see. This is a useful exercise as it encourages you to go deeper into your Mediumship and to look out and around you, rather than using tunnel vision and looking straight ahead.

THERE IS A HUGE VARIETY OF TAROT CARDS AVAILABLE AND TAROT READING CAN BE FUN.

It can be used as an aid to a reading, or as a complete reading, as it provides your client with something to see, and for you both to focus on.

Initially you will find yourself following the meanings of each card as it is written. Eventually as you grow more familiar with your cards, you will add more unseen information given by your Guide, tapping into your intuition and spirituality, giving you more confidence and a blended reading. Remember practice helps you to become more proficient.

Choose the right set of cards for you by picking the set that appeals to you by the colours, words or pictures. Always shuffle the cards between clients and for yourself before a reading.

Follow the instructions given on the pack until you gain confidence and develop your own style of reading.

As always, you are responsible for what you say. You can not blame the cards, because they may be wrongly interpreted by you or your client. Always look for the Light and good in your readings, whatever tool you use.

Remember to observe your client's reaction to the pictures as they may have a different view than yours. Always let your client know that you can focus more or expand on any information you are receiving for the clients clarity.

ORACLE CARDS ARE PICTURE CARDS USUALLY WITH MESSAGES WRITTEN BY THE AUTHOR.

Oracles vary in style as they are up to the artist's impression and your ability to read the card.

Choose the oracle cards you are drawn to, by either choosing the colour or the style of card or the pictures on the cards.

Oracles are a great way of taking the work out of receiving your own message from your guide as it is written on the card, or in the little book that is sometimes provided with the set of oracles.

A three card or nine card spread of Oracle cards can provide you with some simple solutions to your daily life, as can pulling one card out every day.

Start by lining the cards out in sets of three, either as a three set or a nine card spread. Either way will work for you and you will soon develop your favourite way of setting them out.

Take notice of the centre card in a nine card spread, as the centre card is the strongest showing what is happening or could happen with your life now.

These cards will show your past, present, and future, with the past on the left. The present is always the middle card with the future on the right.

AN AURA IS AN ENERGY FIELD THAT SURROUNDS AND ENCLOSES EVERY LIVING THING.

There is an Aura around all objects like a haze.

It can be all the colours of the rainbow and the Aura shines out showing the health and wellbeing or feelings of the person as a shimmering haze around the body.

Good health is sometimes shown as a pale pink, anger as a reddish tone and illness as a grey or pale yellowish colour. You sometimes hear someone say that someone else is looking in the pink today, which means that their aura is giving off a healthy pink energy.

Seeing Auras is relatively simple. Start by looking at something or someone in front of a white or cream coloured wall. Notice how the longer you stare at it, you will see a shimmering haze around it.

Practise with friends and go through the emotions of laughter, fear, anger and feelings of love. Watch the difference and see if you can pick up the extent the Aura moves in and out.

ARE ALL THE SAME, BECAUSE YOU ARE APPROACHING IT THE SAME WAY.

It is all about the intent. It is what you have planned to do and put out to the Universe as I am going to do this.

You will have your client, their Guide and friends and family in spirit and your Guide. It can be a bit disconcerting, doing a phone or zoom reading to have your client's friends and family in Spirit, beside you linking with you and talking to you, at the same time knowing that they are also at your client's place with them.

Should a Medium be paid

The answer to this is yes because it is an exchange of energy. Whether it be monetary or a koha, there should always be an exchange of energy.

The argument against this policy is that mediumship is a gift, the same as healing is a gift and therefore it should be free and you should not charge. This is an old belief .

Although it is your passion and you may have an overwhelming feeling of providing help to others, we live in a monetary society and it is still a job. A good Medium spends the same time and energy as your plumber, electrician, surgeon, etc developing their skills and learning to do their job to the best of their abilities. From a practical point of view, you still have to pay your bills.

To do any job properly, not just mediumship, you train for it and spend hours honing your ability. You are not only using your energy to improve your ability, in many cases the experiences and intensive training that you have followed has involved time and money.

You will find many occasions however, when it feels wrong to charge someone, so follow your gut and don't charge or create a discount for your client. Personally I don't charge for "rescue" readings where the person has had such incorrect information from a reading from someone else, that it has affected their lives to the extent where they have become physically ill or frightened for no valid reason. Always your intuition will help you to decide what to charge in these situations.

SPIRITUAL HEALING

THERE ARE MANY WAYS OF DOING SPIRITUAL HEALING. THE BEST WAY IS THE SIMPLEST WAY.

As with Mediumship, it is a connection to spirit allowing Spirit to use you as a channel to give healing to your client and to yourself. Spiritual healing provides a flow of healing spiritual energy to your client, and as you heal them you receive healing too.

There are rules, of course there are, for the protection of you and your client. Remember that you are not a Doctor, and never give your client advice that many go against medical advice.

If the healing is in a public or Church situation, then ensure that you and your client are in a quiet safe area away from other people, but able to be seen. The reason is for confidentiality and trust and protection for you and your client.

Always ask for Spirit help as you give the healing and have permission from the person that you are giving healing to.

If you are doing Spiritual healing to someone for the first time, introduce yourself to the recipient, and ask them how they are feeling, before you start the healing.

Wash your hands before you start and when you finish. It's good hygiene and provides the intent, saying to Spirit: now I am going to start / finish the healing process.

Explain to your client what you are going to do and what they should expect: a warm feeling on their shoulders.

Begin your healing by standing behind your seated client and holding your hands gently about a couple of centimetres above your clients shoulders, creating a small gap. You may if you wish gently touch your client's shoulders but do not lean on them, or press down heavily.

Tell your client to take a deep breath in and to close their eyes. You may close your eyes if you wish.

Quietly invite Spirit to send healing by going into a meditative state and asking for the most appropriate healing for your client.

The process should take about 5-10 minutes max. It is deep and intense, but is not a cure all and should never be given to replace a Doctor's advice.

During the healing, you may be given advice from Spirit for your client. Use your common sense regarding what you say and how you say it. Remember you are responsible for the words that come out of your mouth, regarding healing and mediumship.

Finish the healing by ensuring your client feels okay and advising them to drink plenty of water over the next little while to assist the ongoing healing. If necessary, and you sense something is wrong then advise your client to perhaps have a checkup with their Doctor.

Try not to frighten them, just find a gentle way to say perhaps a checkup is needed.

ABSENT HEALING IS HEALING THAT IS GIVEN AND SENT BY THOUGHT.

If it is your good intention to send healing to someone who needs it, then you only have to think of their name and they will receive healing from Spirit. It is the only healing that does not require permission from the recipient. Master guides will block any

energy that is not appropriate. It is very strong and it works.

How does it work? You are sending spiritual healing for someone's highest good.

You may also organise with someone to have an absent healing by informing them of the time that you are sending the healing so that they are ready to receive it. When appropriate (using the privacy of your clients details) you could ask other trusted healers to send absent healing to your client.

Reiki and massage both fall under the category of healing. As does Shamanism.

All are useful tools, especially Reiki which may help your mind to focus, enhancing both your Mediumship and healing abilities.

I have previously sent students to take classes in Reiki to help with their focus for Mediumship and Spiritual Healing, to great advantage for them.

Trust and believe that you are making a difference with your healing, because you are! Every time you ask for healing from Spirit for the highest good of your client you make a difference. A group of people all sending healing at the same time, is very powerful.

INTENT (MANIFESTATION)

IT'S ALL ABOUT WHAT YOU WISH FOR IN LIFE AND WHAT YOU WOULD LIKE TO BRING INTO YOUR WORLD. IT IS ALSO ABOUT BELIEVING THAT IT WILL HAPPEN.

The following poem I wrote describes Intent because it is about what you want in life.

Create intent
through thought

The Intent

Be who you are and rejoice in who you are

For you are a wondrous creation

Right up there with the stars, the flowers and all manner of wonderful creations

Rejoice because there you are

You have but one life to lead, and it is up to you

To lead it as you would or should

It is the Intent

It is what you want, mean and feel when you do or try the things that you do

If your intent comes from Spirit, then you will succeed

Aim high and strive to be the best that you can

Try new things, meet new people, make time for you

Feel the joy, feel the laughter, feel the pain

For this is what makes you who you are.

Know that it is Spirit's will for you to feel all of this

And to feel the love and support behind it

It is my intent today to feel Spirit's love and to share it all with you.

ARE EVERYWHERE, HELPING US AND ASSISTING US IN OUR DAILY LIVES.

Are they different from our Guides? The answer is yes. Your Guides are specifically for your help and to advise you in your daily life. Angels are for everyone's help and support. They all come with love.

Angels are described in many religions as God's Messengers, and they each have a different role to play. They are there to help everyone in their own special ways for their highest good.

Welcome them into your life because they are there to help, protect and support you always. Miracles happen with Angels, just ask for their help when you need it, for whatever reason. Safe travels, parking in the best place, health advice, new jobs etc. Anything is possible with an Angel by your side, just ask, trust and believe.

You know when there is an Angel around because you can sense their presence. It is a warm safe feeling of being protected and loved. It is always positive. Angels will often leave a token such as a feather or silver coin in your path, where you know that object should not be there. This is just to show their support and know that you are safe and not alone.

Search for books that will tell you all about Angels and ArchAngels, because there is a huge amount of information. Maybe your path or journey will take you to working closer with the Angels. Above all go with your gut feelings on which Angels to talk to.

One of my favourites is ArchAngel Michael because he is there for protection and help. He is also very practical when things go wrong and a great supporter when things go bump in the night.

PAST LIVES, REINCARNATION AND KARMA

PAST LIVES AND REINCARNATION CAN BE A REALLY CONTROVERSIAL SUBJECT.

You either believe in it or you don't. Personally, I don't believe in past lives for all, and I certainly don't believe that a beautiful soul such as a newborn baby, comes to fix the karmic decisions of a previous lifetime.

I believe in Soul families, where the soul memories as well as the DNA are interconnected and passed down the family. All experiences: fears, passions, deep seated beliefs that you have, all come from an experience that happened to someone generations back, in your family tree.

It's a personal belief, because obviously if you believe in past lives, you therefore believe in reincarnation.

Do I believe that we come here once and the end is the end? No, I believe that you have a choice to come back if you wish, or to go on. That this is not the only Universe that we can come to and that you will still be on your journey no matter where it may take you.

Do I believe in life after life? Yes I do, it's all part of your journey here on earth and in other realms of existence.

I believe that Karma and consequences are part of your experience from birth to death in this lifetime. Some people believe that whatever good or bad things happened to you, or whatever you did to others, comes back to you in your lifetime now, as a consequence or as karma from a previous life.

It all comes down to your own personal belief.

ASTRAL TRAVEL

ASTRAL TRAVEL IS THAT FEELING THAT YOU EXPERIENCE JUST BEFORE WAKING FROM SLEEP OR DAYDREAMING.

It's when your soul takes a journey to other places, and yes in case you're wondering, your Soul always comes back.

When you wake up with a jump it can mean that your soul has come back quickly into your body. This can be an uncomfortable feeling but is not harmful.

You may have memories of being in another place, and can describe it very clearly. Your spiritual awareness will feel clearer and often you will come back with information from your Guides.

Often people will travel on many journeys every night and remember where they have been, and then they will not astral travel for a long while. Some people may never Astral travel or others will Astral travel but not have any awareness of doing so.

CHILDREN OFTEN ARE AWARE OF, AND COMMUNICATE WITH SPIRIT FROM A VERY EARLY AGE.

It's a natural ability and should not be scoffed at, it should be accepted and encouraged.

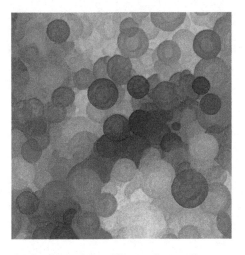

A very young child will sometimes see people there with them that you can not see, or may have an imaginary friend that they play with. They may tell you all sorts of stories of places that their friend tells them about.

Just accept this and always ask kind questions. If the child is not sleeping or becoming upset, then seek a reputable medium or Spiritualist Church.

A reading should not be given to a child or teenager under the age of eighteen.

BLESSING SOMEONE'S HOUSE OR NEW HOME, WORK PREMISES OR LAND TAKES AWAY ANY NEGATIVITY OR SICKNESS THAT CAN BE LINGERING THERE.

It can be done when you are shifting into a new home and is often done when someone has passed to spirit by lifting the energy of the surroundings.

How: By finding the method that suits you. Some people burn white sage to cleanse and bless, some use white light and others simply use a candle to lift the energy. Others use a combination of all three. All of these methods work.

I always send love and healing to the house before I go there and send white light throughout and over the boundaries.

Light a candle in a safe bowl that you can carry and bless each room by walking around. Say a prayer or a mantra as you go. Leave the candle burning for half an hour after you have finished.

Ask Spirit to show you any areas of concern and give extra protection in those areas. Talk to any spirit that may be in the house and tell them what you are doing.

You are cleansing the area of all negativity and sickness allowing new people to live there with love and light.

Remember, simple is best.

It is all about the Intent, and the Intent here is a happy healthy home and all living occupants.

House Blessings… try this blessing. It's one of mine that I use frequently.

Please bless this house and home

Fill it with an abundance of good health and happiness.

Bless all the people and animals that live here

And give love and protection to all who visit here

Bless the earth from boundary to boundary

And may it be abundant.

Allow peace and prosperity to live within these walls

And let these blessings spill over all boundaries to the neighbours

That they may feel your love and blessings also

May the power of your love place protection around this home

And all who live here, live in peace and harmony every day

So, shall it be

FINAL WORD

THIS BOOK IS A COMBINATION OF PARTS OF MY JOURNEY, MY TEACHING AND CONTACT WITH SPIRIT.

This is just touching the surface of my Mediumship journey and Spiritual awareness. I have loved every moment and every tangent that this has taken me on. I have learned that the more I learn and experience,  then there is much more to learn and more opportunities to do so.

My awareness of Spirit is constantly changing, as will yours, and I enjoy learning different ways of linking and working with Spirit.

Above all, love and trust Spirit. Have faith that they will support and help you always.

As a Medium, remember that you do no harm, and that your job and purpose is to help other people every day.

Enjoy your journey, because that is what it is, and love every moment of it, as I do. I hope that this book will provide some insight to you and help you to grow your spiritual awareness and love of life and Spirit.

THANKS FOR READING

I hope you have enjoyed your journey through the pages.

It was a pleasure for me to write these words with the help of Spirit.

I hope that you have gained some inspiration from these words and that they make a difference to your life.

Please look forward to my next book when I can talk to you again through the pages.

Feel free to contact me anytime at jenni@spiritplace.co.nz

Made in the USA
Monee, IL
23 February 2025

12274305R00066